Freestyle Recipes

Complete Guide To Losing Weight And Feeling Great

Sherry S. Williams

Freestyle Recipes: Complete Guide To Losing Weight And Feeling Great

Table of Contents

1 - Introduction

The Freestyle diet takes it to a whole new level by giving zero points to over 200 food that mainly include corn, all types of fish, eggs, seafood, yogurt, chicken breast, turkey breast, lentils, peas, beans, and tofu among others. What this means to say is that the above-mentioned food need not be measured or based on nutritional research, thereby allowing you freedom while losing weight.

The Freestyle diet focuses mainly on eating healthy and more natural food and not just weight loss. SmartPoints put together all complex nutritional information into a single digit. In fact, all fruits and most vegetables contain zero SmartPoints.

The emphasis on comprehensive lifestyle goals is a wise move. There is no such thing as a diet. The kind of lifestyle you lead will always influence how you eat and plays a big role in just about any weight loss program.

2 - Freestyle Breakfast Recipes

Cranberry Soup Bowl

Ingredients:

- 1 cup cranberries

- 4 garlic cloves, chopped

- 5 cups vegetable stock

- 1 orange juice, freshly squeezed

- 5 beets, chopped

- 2 tablespoons coconut sugar

- 1 orange zest

- ½ cup fresh dill fronds, chopped

- Pinch of sea salt

- Pinch of peppercorns

Directions:

1. In a large saucepan, combine garlic, stock, beets, salt, and pepper. Cover the lid and cook on low for 6 hours.

2. Stir in coconut sugar, cranberries, orange juice and zest, and beet leaves. Cover again and cook on high for 30 minutes.

3. Puree the soup in a blender. Transfer to a large soup bowl and chill overnight

4. When ready to use, ladle into individual bowls. Garnish with dill.

Cheesy Egg and Baby Spinach on Toast

Ingredients:

- 3 egg whites, beaten

- ¾ cup baby spinach

- 2 tomato slices

- 2 slices whole wheat bread

- 2 thin slices low-fat cheddar cheese

- 2 tsp. extra virgin olive oil

- 1 ½ tsp. brown mustard

- Black pepper, to taste

Directions:

1. Set the oven to 400 degrees F to preheat.

2. Place a non-stick pan over medium flame and heat through. Once hot, add the olive oil and swirl to coat.

3. Add the egg whites and scramble until cooked to the desired consistency. Then, add the spinach and sprinkle in some pepper. Stir well.

4. Spread the brown mustard on one side of each slice of bread. Then, add the tomato slices on top, followed by the scrambled egg whites.

5. Add the cheese on top, then place the slices on a baking sheet. Bake for 2 minutes or until the cheese melts and the bread is lightly toasted.

6. Transfer to a serving plate and serve right away.

Stir-Fried Broccoli

Ingredients:

- 1 lb broccoli stalks

- 2 garlic cloves, crushed

- 2 black olives

- 3 cups vegetable stock

- Juice of 1 lemon

- ½ silver rind lemon

- Pinch dried chillies

- ½ teaspoon ground coriander

- ½ teaspoon ground cumin

- ½ tablespoons capers

- 2 sun-dried tomatoes

- ½ teaspoon olive brine

- ½ teaspoon caper brine

- Pinch of salt

- Pinch of pepper

Directions:

1. Slice the broccoli stalks into thin rounds.

2. Combine garlic, olives, half the stock, lemon juice,

lemon rind, dried chillies, coriander, cumin, capers, tomatoes, olive brine, and caper brines in a pan. Bring mixture into a boil.

3. Add the broccoli stalks. Pour ½ lemon juice and the remaining stock. Stir-fry broccoli until tender. Season with salt and pepper. Serve.

Shrimp and Leeks Omelet

Ingredients:

- 4 pieces large eggs, whisked

- 2 pieces large garlic cloves, minced

- 2 pieces large leeks, minced, reserve some for garnish

- 2 tablespoons water

- 1 tablespoon olive oil

- 2 pounds frozen cooked shrimps, peeled, minced

- ¼ pound red ripe tomatoes, minced

- Pinch of sea salt

- Pinch of white pepper

- coconut oil for greasing

Directions:

1. Pour oil in a non-stick skillet set over medium heat; sauté garlic and leeks until limp. Add in tomatoes and water; sauté for 2 to 3 more minutes. Add in shrimps; season with salt and pepper. Pour in eggs. Swirl pan around to even out the mixture.

2. Using a fork, push shrimps around to distribute these out; put the lid on. Cook until eggs set completely. Turn off heat.

3. Slice omelet into 4 equal portions, pie-like. Place portions into individual plates. Sprinkle remaining chives on top. Serve.

Prawn and Pea Salad

Ingredients:

- 2 Boston lettuce leaves, rinsed, spun-dried, shredded

For shallots

- 1 shallot, julienned

- Pinch of sea salt

For the Dressing

- ¾ cup mayonnaise

- 1 tablespoon coconut vinegar

- ¼ teaspoon palm sugar, crumbled

- ¼ tablespoon extra-virgin olive oil

- Pinch of sea salt

- Pinch of black pepper to taste

For peas and prawns

- 2 pounds fresh prawns, deveined

- ½ pound frozen peas, thawed

- 2 cups water

- Pinch of sea salt

Directions:

1. Combine shallots and salt in a small bowl; mash using tips of your fingers. Set aside for 15 minutes; rinse

and then drain.

2. Pour water into the saucepan set over high heat. Add a generous pinch of sea salt; boil. Add in prawns and peas. Cook for 10 minutes. Drain. Cool completely to room temperature before tossing into salad.

3. Whisk dressing ingredients in another bowl until well combined. Taste; adjust seasoning if needed.

4. Clean your greens first with this easy-to-use and elegant salad spinner, <u>Oxo Good Grips Salad Spinner</u>. To assemble: place lettuce leaves in a large salad bowl. Add in half of dressing, peas, shallots, and shrimps. Toss well to combine. Place equal portions of salad into plates. Drizzle in more dressing if desired. Serve.

Mexican Egg Scramble

Ingredients:

- 2 egg whites

- 1 egg

- 1 green onion, chopped

- 1 green bell pepper, diced

- 2 Tbsp. unsweetened soy milk

- ground black pepper, to taste

- Olive oil, for greasing

- Hot sauce, to taste

Directions:

1. Lightly coat a skillet with cooking spray and place over medium flame.

2. Once hot, add the tomato, bell pepper, and green onions. Saute until crisp-tender. Transfer to a bowl and set aside.

3. Beat the egg with the egg whites in a bowl then add the soy milk and whisk well. Season with black pepper to taste.

4. Pour the egg mixture into the hot pan and scramble until slightly firm but still moist. Stir the vegetables back into the pan with the eggs.

5. Transfer the egg scramble to a serving dish and serve

right away.

Avocado Spinach Smoothie

Ingredients:

- 1 cup baby spinach

- 1/8 cup fresh pineapple

- ½ avocado, peeled

- 1 tablespoon coconut, shredded

- ½ cup coconut milk

- ½ teaspoon cinnamon

- ¼ teaspoon vanilla extract

Directions:

1. Blend all ingredients in a high power blender until smooth.

2. Pour into a tall glass and serve right away.

Stir-Fried Spinach and Olives

Ingredients:

- 1 lb spinach

- 5 black olives

- 2 garlic cloves, crushed

- Pinch dried chillies

- 2 sun-dried tomatoes

- 1 lemon juice

- ½ silver rind lemon

- ½ teaspoon ground coriander

- ½ teaspoon ground cumin

- ½ teaspoon caper brine

- ½ tablespoons capers

- ½ teaspoon olive brine

- 3 cups vegetable stock

- Pinch of salt

- Pinch of pepper

Directions:

1. Combine garlic, olives, half the stock, lemon juice, lemon rind, dried chillies, coriander, cumin, capers, tomatoes, olive brine, and caper brines in a pan. Bring mixture into a boil.

2. Add the spinach. Pour ½ lemon juice and the remaining stock. Stir-fry spinach until tender. Season with salt and pepper. Serve.

3 - Freestyle Lunch Recipes

Curry Cauliflower and Carrot

Ingredients:

- 2 heads cauliflower, sliced into florets

- 2 carrots, diced

- 1 shallot, minced

- 1 garlic clove, minced

- 1 tablespoon Thai curry paste

- ½ teaspoon turmeric powder

- 2 cups vegetable stock, unsalted

- Pinch of salt

- Pinch of white pepper

- 2 cans 15 oz. each coconut cream, divided

Directions:

1. Pour ingredients into a Dutch oven set over high heat Except for 1 can of coconut cream. Stir. Let sauce boil away until liquid is reduced by half.

2. Pour in the last can of coconut cream. Turn off heat immediately. Taste; adjust seasoning, if needed.

3. Serve on top of boiled/steamed rice, or vegetable noodles with vegan cheese, if desired.

Grilled Miso Shrimp

Ingredients:

- 1 lb. shrimp, deveined, shelled

- 1 tablespoon fresh ginger, grated

- 1 garlic clove, minced

- 3 scallions, cut into 1 ½ inch length

- 2 tablespoons yellow miso

- 3 tablespoons lime juice

- 2 tablespoons vegetable oil

- 1 ½ teaspoon brown sugar

- 1/2 cup Mayonnaise

- 1 tablespoon Sambal oelek

Directions:

1. Pre-heat the grill or grill pan. Meanwhile, whisk vegetable oil, brown sugar, garlic, and 2 tablespoons of lime juice with miso.

2. Add shrimp into the bowl of whisked ingredients to coat. Thread the scallions and the shrimp on an eight-inch skewer.

3. Grill the shrimp over moderate-high heat. Turn once if cooked through and slightly charred. This will take approximately five minutes.

4. In a separate bowl, whisk the sambal oelek and the mayonnaise as well as the remaining lime juice with miso and then serve the shrimp hot and nice in a clean platter. Serve.

Shrimp and Crab Noodles

Ingredients:

- 2 tablespoons coconut oil

- 1 ½ pounds fresh shrimps, deveined

- 1 pack crabsticks, shredded (will serve as noodles)

- 1 pound fresh shiitake mushrooms, sliced thickly

- 1 tablespoon fresh ginger, grated

- 1 shallot, minced

- 4 garlic cloves, minced

- 1 carrot, julienned

- 1 tablespoon light soy sauce

- ¼ pound snow peas

- 1 tablespoon oyster sauce

- ½ tablespoon hoisin sauce

- ½ teaspoon palm sugar, crumbled

- ¼ cup mushroom stock

- Pinch of sea salt

Directions:

1. Pour 1 tablespoon coconut oil into non-stick wok set over medium heat; fry sliced mushrooms until lightly

seared on all sides. Transfer to a plate. Pour remaining oil into the wok, sauté ginger and shallot until limp and aromatic.

2. Add in carrot and mushroom stock; cook until vegetables are crisp-tender, about 4 minutes. Add in shrimps and snow peas; stir-fry until shrimps turn coral.

3. Pour remaining ingredients into the wok; stir-fry to combine. Turn off heat. Adjust seasoning if needed. Ladle equal portions into plates. Serve.

Broccoli with Chicken Livers and Shrimps

Ingredients:

- ½ pound chicken livers, thinly sliced

- 1 head broccoli, sliced into bite-sized florets

- 4 fresh shiitake mushrooms, julienned

- ½ pound frozen shrimps, peeled, thawed, drained

- 2 tablespoon cornstarch, dissolved in...

- 1 tablespoon water

- 1 cup chicken stock, low-sodium

- 1 tablespoon soy sauce

- ¾ cup almond flour, finely milled, add more if needed

- 1 shallot, julienned

- 1 lime, sliced into wedges, for garnish

- Pinch of sea salt

- Pinch of black pepper

- 3 tablespoons coconut oil, divided

Directions:

1. Dredge chicken livers in almond flour until well coated. Pour 2 tablespoons of oil into non-stick wok set over medium heat; fry chicken livers until golden brown.

2. Transfer partially cooked chicken livers to a plate. Stir fry mushrooms in remaining oil until lightly seared; transfer to a plate.

3. Pour remaining oil into wok; sauté shallots until limp and transparent. Pour in chicken stock; boil. Add in broccoli, chicken livers and mushrooms; cook only until broccoli turn one shade brighter, about 5 minutes.

4. Except for lime, add in remaining ingredients. Cook until sauce thickens and shrimps turn coral. Turn off heat. Taste; adjust seasoning if needed.

5. Spoon equal portions into plates; serve with a wedge of lime. Squeeze lime juice over the dish just before eating.

Shrimps and Kale on Zucchini Noodles

Ingredients:

Kale, shrimps, and seasonings

- 1 pound fresh shrimps, deveined

- ½ pound fresh kale leaves, shredded

- 3 tablespoons olive oil

- ¾ tablespoon five-spice powder

- Pinch of sea salt

- Pinch of black pepper

For the Salad

- 1 carrot, julienned

- 1 zucchini, processed into spaghetti noodles

- 1 ginger, julienned

- 1 onion, julienned

- 3 tablespoons sesame oil

- 1 lime, sliced into wedges

- ¼ cup rice wine vinegar

Directions:

1. Pour 2 tablespoons of olive oil into wok set over high heat. Sauté shrimps with salt, five spice powder, and pepper; cook until shrimps turn coral. Transfer cooked pieces into a salad bowl.

2. Pour remaining olive oil into the same wok; add in kale leaves and a small pinch of salt. Cook until leaves

wilt. Place kale leaves on top of shrimps; cool before adding in remaining ingredients.

3. Process your zucchini into pasta strands with <u>Paderno World Cuisine 6-Blade Vegetable Slicer</u>. This will definitely be your partner in making healthy and visually appealing meals.

4. Place remaining ingredients into a salad bowl. Toss well to combine; spoon equal portions into plates. Taste; adjust seasoning if needed. Serve.

Whole Wheat Chicken Pasta

Directions:

- 4 chicken breasts, boneless, skinless

- Pinch of salt

- Pinch of pepper

- 4 garlic cloves, minced

- 1 cup mushrooms, sliced

- 2 tablespoons flour

- 1 tablespoon butter

- ½ teaspoon dried thyme

- 1 cup chicken broth

- 2 tablespoons balsamic vinegar

- 2 tablespoons olive oil

Directions:

1. Season chicken breasts with salt and pepper. Place flour in a bowl. Coat the chicken breasts with flour.

2. Heat the oil in a pan over medium heat. Add the chicken and sauté for about four minutes. Stir in the garlic and mushrooms.

3. Stir in thyme, broth, and the balsamic vinegar. Cook for another seven minutes. Add the butter and pour the sauce to the chicken.

4. Divide the dish among five microwaveable containers. Place the containers in the refrigerator and microwave when you're ready to eat.

4 - Freestyle Dinner Recipes

Sweet and Sour Chicken

Ingredients:

Chicken

- 2 pounds chicken breast fillets

- 1 tablespoon Spanish paprika

- 1 tablespoon onion powder

- 1 tablespoon garlic powder

- Pinch of sea salt

- Pinch of white pepper

Batter

- 1 egg, whisked

- ¼ cup self-rising flour

- 2 cups almond flour, finely milled

- ¼ cup cornstarch

- 1 cup cold water

- ⅛ teaspoon baking powder

Stir-fry

- 1 teaspoon coconut oil

- 2 garlic cloves, minced

- 2 onions, quartered

- 1 red bell pepper, cubed

- 1 green bell pepper, cubed

- Pinch of sea salt

Sauce

- 1 carrot, sliced into flowers

- 1 can pineapple tidbit, juices included

- 2 tablespoons lime juice, freshly squeezed

- 2 tablespoons sugar, crumbled

- 1 teaspoon cornstarch, dissolved in 1 cup water

- ½ cup rice wine vinegar

- Pinch of sea salt

- Pinch of white pepper

- Olive oil

Directions:

1. Place chicken ingredients in a food-safe bag; seal. Check out and try this <u>Airsunny Clear Resealable Cello</u>, a food grade safe, thicker, and stronger than other food-safe bags. Massage contents of the bag to mix; chill in the fridge for at least 30 minutes (or up to 48 hours beforehand.) Drain well the chicken prior to use; discard marinade.

2. Whisk batter ingredients in a bowl until smooth; add more water if flour clumps together, but you need a thick, pancake-like batter for this recipe. Add in chicken; stir until meat is well coated.

3. Half fill the deep fryer with oil; set over medium heat. When oil becomes slightly smoky, slide in a few breaded chicken cubes at a time; cook until golden brown. Place cooked meat on a platter lined with paper towels. Set aside.

4. Pour coconut oil into non-stick wok set over medium

heat. Stir-fry garlic and onions until latter turns transparent. Add in remaining stir-fry ingredients, plus cooked chicken. Cook until bell peppers are limp and aromatic. Remove wok from heat.

5. Mix cornstarch and ¼ cup of water together in a bowl. Except for lime juice, pour remaining sauce ingredients in a saucepan set over high heat. Bring to boil; reduce heat to lowest setting. Cook partially covered until carrots are fork-tender. Pour in cornstarch slurry and lime juice; whisk until sauce thickens. Turn off heat.

6. Off heat, pour sauce into stir-fry when you are ready to serve; toss to combine. Taste; adjust seasoning if needed. Place equal portions into plates; serve.

Grilled Spiced Tofu

Ingredients:

- 28 oz extra firm tofu, drained well

- 1 teaspoon chili garlic paste

- 1 ½ tablespoons pure maple syrup

- 1 tablespoon soy sauce, low sodium

- 1 garlic clove, minced

- Pinch of ground black pepper

- Coconut oil

Directions:

1. Slice the tofu into large cubes and place between two sheets of paper towels. Press gently with a flat plate until most of the water is squeezed out.

2. Combine the remaining ingredients in a bowl and season with ground pepper. Then, add the tofu. Turn several times to coat.

3. Cover the bowl with plastic wrap, then refrigerate for at least 4 hours, preferably overnight, to marinate.

4. Once the marinated tofu cubes are ready, place a grill pan over medium-high flame and heat through. Once hot, coat with coconut oil.

5. Grill the tofu for about 5 minutes, turning occasionally and basting with the marinade.

6. Transfer to a serving dish. Serve.

Fish Tofu Stir-Fry

Ingredients:

- 2 garlic cloves, minced

- 1 white onion, minced

- 1 ½ pounds shrimp

- ¼ pound French beans

- 1 tablespoon olive oil

- 1 package fish tofu, halved

- Pinch of sea salt

Cornstarch Slurry

- 1 tablespoon cornstarch

- ¼ cup water

- 1 tablespoon oyster sauce

- ¼ teaspoon palm sugar, crumbled

Directions:

1. Season shrimps with salt. Place in a bowl.

2. Mix cornstarch slurry in another bowl until sugar dissolves.

3. Pour oil into non-stick wok set over high heat; sauté garlic and onion until limp and transparent.

4. Add in fish tofu and shrimps; stir-fry until latter turns coral. Add in remaining ingredients, including cornstarch slurry; cook until sauce thickens and French beans turn a shade brighter, about 3 minutes. Turn off heat immediately. Taste; adjust seasoning if needed. Spoon equal portions into plates; serve.

Chili Corn Bean Beef

Ingredients:

*   1 Serrano chile, finely chopped

*   1 green pepper, chopped

*   1 tablespoon chili powder

*   1 ½ cups corn,

- 15 ounces pinto beans

- ½ pound beef, ground, extra-lean

- 1 onion, finely chopped

- 2 teaspoons cumin

- 15 ounces tomatoes, crushed

Directions:

1. Coat a large nonstick skillet with cooking spray.

2. Add the onion, chile pepper, and green pepper. Saute for 2 minutes or until the onions have softened.

3. Stir in cumin and chili powder. Cook for 2 minutes or until fragrant. Crumble the ground beef into the skillet and cook for 5 minutes or until cooked through.

4. Add corn, pinto beans, and tomatoes. Stir well to combine. Allow simmering for 10 to 15 minutes. Serve immediately.

Tomato Eggplant Salad

Ingredients:

- 12 slices thick eggplant

- 6 slices thick tomato

- 6 pieces of fresh basil leaves

- 6 pieces fresh portabella mushroom caps

- 4 tablespoons lime juice, freshly squeezed

- 2 tablespoons fresh parsley, minced, for garnish

- extra virgin olive oil

- Pinch of sea salt

- Pinch of black pepper

Directions:

1. Lightly grease non-stick skillet with oil; set over medium heat. Fry aubergine until browned well.

2. Transfer to a plate; do same for mushrooms and tomatoes. Season these with lime juice, pepper, and salt.

3. Stack veggie salad in this order: aubergine slice, mushroom cap, tomato slice, basil leaf, and another

aubergine slice.

4. Sprinkle a small amount of parsley on top. Drizzle more olive oil and salt on top if desired. Serve.

5 - Conclusion

With the Freestyle Diet, you are offered more food options although it steers you toward healthier options.

This kind of diet isn't much of a diet program but more of a lifestyle. All you have to do is be mindful of what you're eating, track your choices of food, be active at all times, and know the ingredients you put in your food.

When you follow this diet, no food is forbidden, but of course, you always have to go for the healthier choices.

Thank You

As we reach the end of this book, I want to say thanks for reading this book.

I want to get this information out to as many people as possible. If you found this book helpful, I would greatly appreciate you leaving me a review. This helps others find the book as well.

Disclaimer

This document is geared towards providing exact and reliable information in regards to the topic and issue covered. The publication is sold on the idea that the publisher is not required to render an accounting, officially permitted, or otherwise, qualified services. If advice is necessary, legal, financial, medical or professional, a practiced individual in the profession should be ordered.

This information is not presented by a financial or medical practitioner and is for entertainment, educational and informational purposes only. The content is not intended as a substitute for professional medical advice, diagnosis, or treatment. Always seek the advice of your physician or other qualified health care provider with any questions you may have regarding a medical condition. Never disregard professional medical advice or delay in seeking it because of something you have read.

The information provided herein is stated to be truthful and consistent, in that any liability, in terms of inattention or otherwise, by any usage or abuse of any policies, processes, or directions contained within is the solitary and utter responsibility of the recipient reader. Under no circumstances will any legal responsibility or blame be held against the

DISCLAIMER

publisher for any reparation, damages, or monetary loss due to the information herein, either directly or indirectly.

Last Updated: 16.Aug.2018

www.ingramcontent.com/pod-product-compliance
Lightning Source LLC
Chambersburg PA
CBHW071256130726
47998CB00003B/1213